THE SPIRIT O]
CRICH
WHATSTANDWELL, FRITCHLEY
& SURROUNDING AREAS

Ken Jackson

Published by

Landmark Publishing Ltd
Ashbourne Hall, Cokayne Ave, Ashbourne, Derbyshire DE6 1EJ England
Tel: (01335) 347349 Fax: (01335) 347303
e-mail: landmark@clara.net
website: www.landmarkpublishing.co.uk

ISBN 1 84306 147 3

© **Ken Jackson 2004**

British Library Cataloguing in Publication Data: a catalogue
record for this book is available from the British Library.

Print: Bath Press, Bath
Design: Mark Titterton
Cover: James Allsopp

Front cover: Crich Cross and villagers, 1913

Title page: Market Place with children.

Back cover top: Track up to the Stand.

Back middle: Public works helped the unemployment situation after World War I

Back cover bottom: Whatstandwell Railway Station, 1907

LANDMARK COLLECTOR'S LIBRARY

THE SPIRIT OF
CRICH
WHATSTANDWELL, FRITCHLEY & SURROUNDING AREAS

Ken Jackson

Landmark Publishing

Contents

Introduction

In 2003 the Crich Heritage Partnership set out to create a computer archive of old photographs covering the parish of Crich. The parish embraces Whatstandwell, Fritchley, Bull Bridge, Wheatcroft, Wakebridge and Plaistow Green as well as Crich itself. With the kind loan of photo collections from people with roots in the area, the archive began to grow and is still open for the inclusion of additional images. The Partnership would welcome any offers from people with interesting material.

The 'Awards for All' arm of the Lottery distributors supported the archive project with a generous grant.

Whilst our Crich heritage of images is available to those who are happy using computers, we recognise that many people feel more comfortable with the printed page. And so the idea of a book was born and the Partnership is pleased to have collaborated with Landmark Publishing in the production of this volume. It draws on the archive of pictures to create a nostalgic look at this unique locality. Perched on the southernmost hill of the Derbyshire Pennines, Crich has had a long history as men came to exploit its minerals and its stone. In doing so they left their mark on the landscape and settled wherever a spring of water came to the surface. The resulting scatter of gritstone settlements and the lofty hill, visible for miles, give the parish its special character. Photographers came to capture pictures of the picturesque corners and the wider views of Crich Hill and the towers that have marked its summit. So the surviving pictures from the 19th and 20th centuries form the basis of our book and, inevitably, they show how much has already changed as the area grows and prospers.

The Partnership hope it brings pleasure to its readers and encourages everyone with an interest in the parish to value its past and help conserve what is best.

Acknowledgments

I wish to thank the following people for sharing their photographic collections and thus allowing the production of this book: Les Barber, Beryl Calladine, Geoff Dawes, Brian Key, Alan Rimmer, Stan Smith and Helen Whitmore. Alan Flint and Brian Key helped with proof-reading. My personal thanks go to my wife, Val without whom this book would literally not have been written.

Ken Jackson
July 2004

The oldest part of Crich clusters around the church. There was probably a settlement on this hilltop before the church was built. In the foreground are the worked-out faces of Cliff Quarry.

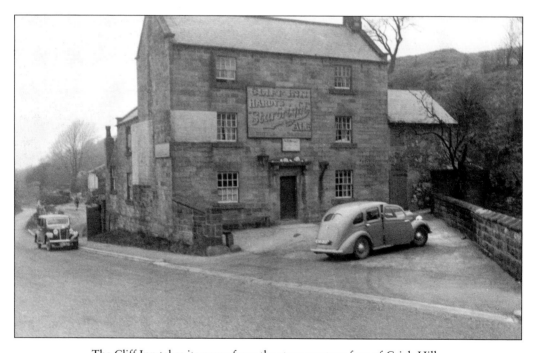

The Cliff Inn takes its name from the steep western face of Crich Hill.

Lead miners, quarry workers and lime burners at the kilns must all have patronised the Cliff Inn and its predecessors.

The Stand dominates the highest point of the parish but the church and the village core sit nearby on a lower knoll of the limestone dome which underlies Crich.

Above: Town End. Houses face across Cromford Road to the churchyard. The inn sign for the Bulls Head can be seen at top left.

Right: Town End. Many of the elements in this late 19th century view still remain.

Below: A similar view to the preceding one but with a pen and colour wash to increase postcard sales.

St. Mary's Church - the oldest building in the village with simple Norman arches as its dominant interior feature. The tower, spire and south aisle date from the 14th century.   *G. Smith*

Original masonry dating from about 1150 comprises the north and south arcades of the nave. The south aisle was added in about 1320. The nave was raised in the Perpendicular period, around 1400.

Above: Old tracks radiate out from the church, giving access to the fields. Sheep graze in the Holywell fields.

Right: Early summer with the fields between Coast Hill and the church ready for mowing.

Below: A 'Christmas card' scene with the church and cemetery under snow.

Above: The higher part of the village taken from The Jubilee, a popular viewpoint for photographers. The gritstone outcrops alongside Sandy Lane are seen in contrast to the limestone exposures of Cliff Quarry.

Right: A winter photo from The Jubilee allows a good view of the derelict quarry between Wheatsheaf Lane and Jeffries Lane.

Below: The photographer braves the elements to preserve this wintry scene from the 1930s.

Left: Crich Cross in the 1920s surrounded by a very bleak-looking group of buildings which include the smithy on the left.

Below: The Cross, the Jovial Dutchman Inn and a very rutted road.

The Cross in the early 1900s with village children. In 1871 funds were raised to restore the village cross on its old base. This is the result but no-one knows what happened to its predecessor.

The Jovial Dutchman has had a smart facelift in this picture and boasts a handsome swinging sign. Inset the same scene taken about 1913 with an obliging group of villagers.

Above: A postcard sent out to France in World War I. The sender identifies the horse and dray as belonging to the Co-op.

Left: An excess of zeal for signposts by the County Council which thankfully was short-lived.

Below: The former Greyhound Inn on Roe's Lane. In 1846 the innkeeper was Joseph Roe.

Bowns Hill in the 1950s before it was widened.

The Black Swan around 1950. Previously it operated as a coaching inn on the Nottingham to Newhaven turnpike road established in the 1760s.

The Market Place and Bulling Lane with a surprising amount of grass surviving into the early 20th century.

Another picture from the early 20th century with a gas lamp providing a focal point. Gas street lighting came to Crich in 1921.

The Market Place troughs have a stone pavement in front to take the wear and tear of animals, otherwise the surface is completely unmetalled.

A view from the 1950s showing the archway of the mineral railway built in 1840-41. Beyond are the former council houses built in 1949-50.

Above: This view of the Market Place is dominated by the Baptist Chapel built in the late 1870s.

Left: By the 1950s the troughs had begun to attract all sorts of "street furniture".

Above: The former Post Office on the south side of the Market Place as it was in 1908 when it was managed by Miss Mary Ann Higton.

Right: Benefiting from its central location the village store, seen here in the 1960s, has had a long life under various owners.

Below: The village Post Office had been relocated when this picture was taken around 1960.

Right: The Blount Store and Tea Rooms around 1920.

Above: The south end of the Market Place with the bakery, which still survives.

Right: The same area viewed from Rosskeen in May 1959.

Left: "Remember thy time; all flesh must die" - a wonderful memento mori at Dimple Green.

Below: The Rising Sun with gleaming new paintwork. It closed in 1977.   *G. Smith*

Left: Rosskeen was home to the medical practices of Doctors G. G. McDonald and H. J. Rankin seen here in 1907. Dr. McDonald's daughter, always known as 'Dr. Eileen' took over the practice in 1935 on the death of her father.

This, and the previous picture, show that the Bottomside and the Topside were linked for vehicles by a sloping connection. Note the oil lamp with a wrought iron arch.

An arresting picture of Sun Lane under deep snow in the 1950s.

A recent picture of the former Primitive Methodist Chapel in Sun Lane which, because of its tucked-away location and cramped site, never makes it into photo collections.

Left: The Parish Room before its conversion into a private house.

Below: A wonderful picture of everyday life around 1920 at the bottom of Bennetts Lane.

Left: Lots of interesting detail in this view from The Tors taken in the early part of the 20th century. The mounds in the foreground comprise spoil from the parish quarry and doubtless from the driving of the railway tunnel under The Jubilee.

Top: Looking east from The Tors Steps in about 1970.

Above: Tors Steps themselves, looking west. Probably an old route out of the village which demanded to be saved from the encroaching quarry workings to either side.

Right: A view from The Tors taken in the summer of 1965 showing the houses on Culland View under construction.

Above: This 19th century picture shows that the Kings Arms has a long history of serving the village.

Left: The Wesleyan Methodist Chapel. Built in 1765, the chapel was visited in March 1766 by John Wesley himself. He preached to "a loving, simple-hearted people".

Below: Crich Common at the foot of Chapel Lane. A bike is the only wheeled vehicle in sight.

"Workhouse Row", the former poorhouse for Crich and several other parishes including Pentrich and Wessington. It is recorded as having been built in 1734.

Crich Common near the former police station (built 1901). The main roads through the village were not metalled until the 1920s.

An unusual view of Crich taken from Thorp Hill, Fritchley in February 1981.

The Briars Residential Centre between Crich and Fritchley built in 1907.

The Briars in the early 1900s showing its relationship with Crich Common.

The Briars, was run by the Ludlows, a Quaker family, as a guest house with a strict vegetarian regime.

Crich Stand, sited at 286m above sea level, has had many forms over the centuries but
has always been both a landmark and a viewpoint. The Cliff Inn is on the right.

Over many years the Cliff Quarry has been worked with a prominent west face, creating a rich haul of
pure limestone and generating mounds of quarry waste.

This picture shows very clearly the anticline or dome of Carboniferous limestone strata which makes up Crich Hill.

Crich limestone has been worked and transported round the country since medieval times and Cliff Quarry has survived (with some breaks in production) to the present day. The summit of Crich Hill has, in effect, been chopped in two over the centuries.

In 1840 much of this land had been bought or leased by George Stephenson, the Victorian entrepreneur. Once his railway line reached the quarry limestone production increased greatly.

Replacing a conical predecessor, this simple stone tower was built in 1851 by Francis Hurt of Alderwasley at a cost of £210.

Crich Stand (1851-1922) with a flight of steps on the south side of its sturdy plinth.

Left: Taken around 1880, this photograph incorporates a couple of people to give scale to the structure. A fence indicates the quarry area on the left.

Below: A fascinating picture from the end of the 19th century showing the old track up to the Stand. It confirms just how close the quarry face had come to the former tower.

By 1882 the expansion of stone production had brought the quarry face to within a few metres of the Stand. Lightning strikes had taken their toll on the structure.

Right: In July 1882 a landslip to the west of the Stand sealed its fate. In the interests of public safety the tower was closed and the fence was moved from the west of the tower to the east.

Below: This postcard purports to show the traces of the landslide which made slow but awful progress down the flank of the hill demolishing several cottages and displacing the road several metres to the west.

Some years later the scars had begun to heal.

To commemorate the men of the Sherwood Foresters Regiment who died in the First World War it was decided to build a beacon memorial on Crich Hill. Stone from the 'Hurt' tower, donated by the Clay Cross Company, was removed in 1922 and numbered for use in the rebuilding.

The Stand which we know today, looking very pristine. It was erected by Joseph Payne, a Crich builder. The site had been granted by the Hurt family of Alderwasley.

An early postcard captures the quiet dignity of the newest Derbyshire landmark.

A large crowd turns out to attend the official opening on 6th August 1923. The ceremony was performed by General Sir Horace Smith-Dorrien, Colonel of the Sherwood Foresters, who had himself seen service in France.

An atmospheric shot of the new memorial showing the old road which then served both the tower and the new warden's bungalow.

In time a new road was constructed to give better access and was much appreciated by those making the pilgrimage to the memorial. In 1934 a revolving searchlight was installed in the tower.

The southern end of Cliff Quarry was worked-out and grown over when this picture was taken around 1930. The active quarry area had moved north and was producing 50,000 tons per year.

Left: A view from the west showing the increase of tree cover on Cliffside.

Below: This early 1960s photograph shows the southernmost part of Cliff Quarry after its closure and takeover by the Tramway Museum Society. The quarry buildings and rail track beds have a new life as storage and workshops for a clutch of rescued trams.

Right: A picture from the early 1960s which shows the beginnings of the Museum as a public attraction. Funds raised from visitors go back into restoring and adding to the collection of trams.

Above: An August Bank Holiday event in 1969 indicates the growing ambition and organising abilities of the Tramway Museum Society.

Above: A fine aerial picture from 1987 shows the limestone working sweeping to the northeast of the Stand. A haulage road clings to the bottom of the old cliff face. The rest of the former quarry is occupied by the much-extended attractions of the Tramway Village.

Right: A carpet of snow smoothes out the blemishes of the quarry floor.

George Stephenson built this narrow-gauge railway in 1840-41 to exploit the limestone of Crich Hill and transport it three kilometres to lime kilns at Ambergate. This picture shows loaded stone wagons pulled by the little steam engine 'DOWIE' in about 1900.

The 'Coffeepot' locomotive 'TOMMY' is seen at work in Cliff Quarry around 1910. The name 'TOMMY' was later transferred to an 0-4-0 tank locomotive purchased in 1924. This latter engine worked on the line until the end of steam traction, around 1953.

This photograph gives a good indication of how the quarry was worked, with successive feeder lines from the face joining the main spine railway.

Here the main feeder tracks converge at the site of the present Tramway Village before leaving the quarry via a low bridge under the Matlock road.

The engine shed is seen on the left with workshops to its rear where the wagons were built and repaired.

A better view of the workshops at Cliff Quarry, but showing haulage being carried out by diesel locomotives, introduced in 1952.   *A. Rimmer*

The line ran southward from Cliff Quarry and negotiated several bridges before passing under The Jubilee in a sixty metre tunnel through the millstone grit.

Above: The line ran along the foot of The Tors and crossed Chadwick Nick Lane by an ungated level crossing. This picture from 1956 shows a diesel and eleven loaded wagons heading for Bowmer Rough.   *A. Rimmer*

Right: From Bowmer Rough to the Ambergate kilns a drop of 25 metres down the side of the Amber Valley was involved at a 1 in 4 gradient. Stephenson designed a self-acting incline whereby the weight of loaded wagons going down the slope pulled up empty wagons on a parallel track.   *A. Rimmer*

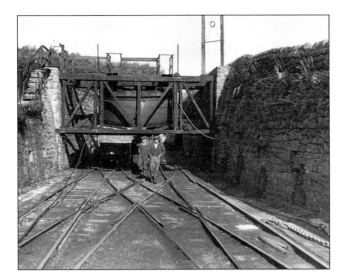

Left: The incline became known as The Steep and control was maintained by a large winding drum with a hand-operated brake.   *A. Rimmer*

Below: Accidents did occur but usually the loaded wagons got safely to the bottom of the valley to serve the lime kilns.

The Ambergate kilns achieved their peak production in 1937-38 burning over 73,000 tons of stone, fuelled by coal from Wingfield Manor Colliery. George Stephenson had originally developed the complex of quarries, railways and kilns and his company became the Clay Cross Company in 1851.

Taken out of use in the 1950s the steam locomotives were kept under canvas sheets for some years. Here is the second TOMMY with Town End in the background.   *A. Rimmer*

Left: Cliff Quarry closed in May 1957 and with it the mineral railway. Dene Quarry at Cromford supplied stone to the limeworks but they too closed in October 1965.

Below: This handsome little engine, called 'FITZ' was built for The Butterley Company by W. G. Bagnall of Stafford in 1894.

Below: The other mineral railway in the parish is remembered by fewer people because it closed earlier, in the winter of 1932-33, after operating since 1793. At first it used horse power but from about 1860, locomotives. This scene shows the walled embankment through Fritchley.

Right: The Old Quarry was closed in the early 20th century but Hilts continued until 1933. The last chapter in the story was the cutting-up of the wagons near the Hat Factory in 1936.

Above: A marvellous view which shows the Hat Factory with the Gangroad running in front of it to reach the Warner or Old Quarry and a new branch striking up to the already sizeable Hilts Quarry.

Right: A short-lived railway operated in Bilberry Wood to take gritstone from a new nearby quarry to the construction site for a new reservoir built by the Derwent Valley Board in 1906-1910.

Fritchley straggles down the hillside from Crich Common to the brook. Like most villages its origins were based on agriculture but its specific location is due to good supplies of spring water.

The village has always had a traditional green and for the most part this survives to the present day.

Above: Built in a simple Classical style, the Congregational Chapel was opened in 1841. This photo of 1908 shows stone drinking troughs very like those at Crich Market Place. The Fritchley troughs have not survived.

Left: Across the Green from the Chapel stood the grocery and draper's shop run by Thomas Davidson, a local Quaker minister. Next door, with a pony and trap in attendance, is the local butcher's shop of F. J. Lynam.

Right: A pony and trap give added interest to this close-up of Davidson's village shop.

Davidson's shop was the original village post office but in the early 1900s it moved to new accommodation and was run by the Lynam family for many years.

The Quakers, or more correctly The Society of Friends, have been a significant presence in Fritchley since the 17th century. Meetings were held originally in the private houses of Friends but in 1897 the Friends Meeting House was opened on Chapel Street.

Local children are being posed to have their picture taken in this view with the Red Lion on the far left. The two cottages, one thatched, were demolished to accommodate the Red Lion as it is now.

Bobbin Mill Hill levels-out to cross the Fritchley Brook at the lowest point of the village street. Chestnut Bank House was built by Edward Watkins, a local mill-owner, in the 1880s. The Society of Friends ran a private school at the house from 1885 to the late 1920s.

A wider view of the lower village shows Fernside - the large white house on the right. The stone cottage below it was used for the Fritchley Meeting of the Society of Friends before the Meeting House was built.

A pony and trap tackles the rutted and stoney track which is now Lynam Road.

This panoramic view shows a swathe of the village from Kirkham Lane and the Gangroad in the foreground to Bowmer Rough Farm and the bare skyline of the new reservoir in the background.

The ruins of the windmill near Lynam Road viewed from the west. The mill went out of use in 1817 and has been crumbling ever since.

Whatstandwell

Over the centuries the scattered farming hamlets of Coddington, Crich Carr and Whatstandwell Bridge have coalesced to form what is now known as Whatstandwell - seen here from Alderwasley Park.

The scatter of houses on the east bank of the River Derwent was formerly all known as Crich Carr. It is said that only the area west of the canal is truly Whatstandwell !

A view from the southwest which shows Chase Cliffe House at the top right with the hamlet of Thurlow Booth below it in the woods which were formerly part of Crich Chase – a manorial hunting reserve.

The local geography squeezes together the communication routes near Whatstandwell giving rise to the famous juxtaposition of river, road, rail and canal. In the background are Shining Cliff Woods.

A view near Whatstandwell Bridge showing the Derwent Hotel. The field in the middle foreground used to accommodate tents, caravans and shanty homes for visitors. During the Second World War families who had been 'bombed out' in Sheffield made their temporary home here.

Whatstandwell Bridge. The first bridge was built here in 1390 by John de Stepul of Steeple Grange near Wirksworth. It replaced an earlier ford.

The A6 as it used to be in the early years of the 20th century. The photographer probably waited ages for a motor car to appear.

A view taken in the 1940s with more traffic on the A6. By this time the canal, uphill from the river, was out of operation.

Left: The North Midland Railway came into this part of the Derwent Valley in 1849. A first Whatstandwell Station was built in 1853 just to the north of the Derwent Hotel but was replaced by this handsome stone building in 1894. The original station buildings were demolished but the platform still remains.

Left: This view from 1907 shows the splendid foot-bridge over the lines. As well as serving local people, the station was an important point of entry for visitors who were met by carriages and ferried to local attractions or inns.

Left: An early picture of the timber-clad signal box at Whatstandwell which stood near the former station site. It controlled sidings which served the Dukes Quarries and the goods yard.

Left: The Cromford Canal was built through Crich Parish in 1794. This postcard view from about 1930 shows the bridge carrying the Crich road over the canal.

Below: A view of the village from Edwardian times as a laden cart negotiates the steep gradient. Round Wood graces the skyline.

Right: A similar view in the 1940s. The roof of the Wheatsheaf pub boasts its brewery identification in large letters.

Right: Curious village children are captured in this shot which depicts Main Road before it was metalled.

Below: Higher up the hill substantial gritstone houses face out over the Derwent Valley. Local people will remember the impressive springs of water which cascaded out of the rock faces to the rear of some of the properties.

Left: Cottages on Middle Lane, Whatstandwell in the early years of the 20th century.

Left: Another quiet, domestic scene from Whatstandwell in the 1930s. These cottages are at the foot of Shaws Hill.

An architect's perspective drawing of the proposed chapel on Carr Lane, drawn in 1877.

Above: Chase Cliffe House built in 1860 as the home for the three spinster sisters Emma, Elizabeth and Selina Hurt who became great benefactresses around the parish.

Right: Dawbarns Factory and the hamlet of Robin Hood to its rear. A stone sawmill was built here to process gritstone from the quarries and Robin Hood came into existence in the 19th century to house workers in the ten quarries and the sawmill.

This view in the late 1920s was taken from the Crich Council footbridge. It shows Eden House at Whatstandwell on the Cromford Canal.

Left: In the far north of Crich Parish, where six old tracks (now footpaths) used to converge, stands Shuckstone Cross - or rather a cross base. Was this just a guidepost on a lonely stretch of moorland or do the enigmatic carvings carry some message other than directions ?

Below: A summertime view of Wakebridge Manor Farm. It is likely that a settlement has occupied the head of this gentle valley for over a thousand years. Lord of the manor, William de Wakebridge, gave money to Crich Church in memory of family members who died of the Black Death in 1349.

The Duke of Devonshire's estates spread way beyond the core area at Chatsworth and formerly included the area between Whatstandwell and Holloway. This curving bridge separates the 'Wild Common' on the right from the hamlet of Robin Hood.

Gregory Wide Hole on the Cromford Canal between Holloway and Robin Hood. The canal was designed to hug the contours of the Derwent Valley but not sufficiently to remove the need for a substantial embankment.

Near to Ambergate the canal narrowed under Chase Bridge - a good place to insert stop planks, either to pond-back water to keep levels up for navigation or to de-water a length for maintenance.

In this view the stop planks have been removed from their rack and inserted in slots near the bridge to retain water.

Above: The Canal features strongly again in this general view of Bull Bridge. The picture probably dates from the 1920s when new elevators had been built at the Butterley Company lime kilns.

Left: The Canal crossed the Ambergate-Ripley road on a stone aqueduct (seen here from the Ripley side) built in the 1790s by Benjamin Outram.

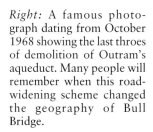

Right: A famous photograph dating from October 1968 showing the last throes of demolition of Outram's aqueduct. Many people will remember when this road-widening scheme changed the geography of Bull Bridge.

The Amber is not a large river but it has been known to rise rapidly and cause local havoc. This picture was taken in September 1931.

Several feet of flood water swirl through the Lord Nelson car park in 1931.

A photo from the 19th century shows the toll bars and cottage by the Hurt Arms. A legacy of turnpike roads established in 1817, these features had all disappeared by 1904. The Cromford and Belper Turnpike Trust was formed to build a new road along the Derwent Valley.

A heavily retouched postcard of Ambergate's famous triangular station looking north-west towards Johnson's Wireworks. The line swinging away to the right went to Sheffield and was opened in 1840 whilst the line heading on up the Derwent Valley was not completed until 1849.

Left: A closer view of the station with soldiers posing at the southern end of the triangular platforms. The occasion is thought to be the railway workers strike of 1911.

In this view the station platforms have escaped the flood but the Hurt Arms is suffering.

The area where the River Amber flows into the River Derwent has been a flooding trouble-spot over the years. This picture from the 1930s shows traffic at a standstill on the A6.

The Bottom Hagg, a well-used footpath from Allen Lane, Fritchley to Ambergate. The lower length of
the footpath can still be negotiated but it lost much of its charm when it was diverted around the fenced
compound of the new gas plant in the mid 1960s.

An intriguing picture from the early 1920s showing an out-of-the-way part of the parish which would
never have been photographed except for a char-a-banc accident.

Crich probably owes its origins to the extraction of lead from surface deposits in Roman times. Over the centuries the miners went deeper and deeper in search of ore. The Wakebridge Mine went to a depth of 200 metres and steam engines were introduced. This view, towards Windy Gap, shows visitors to the derelict site in late Victorian times.

The Old End lead mine closed in 1864 and this picture, taken 100 years later, shows the remaining stonework of the engine house. The shaft was dug entirely through the carboniferous limestone and went to a depth of about 280 metres below the surface.

Left: Another mainstay of the local economy has always been agriculture, particularly pastoral farming because of the parish's height above sea-level. This scene shows the cattle market traditionally held three or four times each year in the vicinity of the church.

Below: A familiar picture showing the farming community trading in sheep – probably at the October Fair. After World War I the market declined in importance and was last held in the 1920s.

A picture of the Lynam family of Tithe Farm, Fritchley having a well-earned rest from haymaking.

Gritstone was extracted from many places in the parish, notably The Tors. This photo from the 1920s shows workers at one of the ten quarries which made up the Dukes Quarries near Whatstandwell. Originally the stone was shipped-out from a wharf on the Cromford Canal, but was later transported on the railway.

A romantic picture, probably from the 1870s, of the derelict windmill and cottage near Lynam Road, Fritchley one of the four or five windmills that the parish once supported. Rather strangely a photograph of 1880 shows the mill having deteriorated further but a new pantile roof on the miller's cottage.

A picture from the early 1950s showing a happy bunch of workers at Cliff Quarry, Crich.

Limestone quarrying to extract 'Crich lime', famous for its high quality, operated on a large scale and made enormous changes to the appearance of the district. Hilts Quarry crept very close to the heart of the village before it was closed in 1933.

The keystone at the outlet of Fritchley Sough shows a carved date of 1753 and although difficult to get to, it remains a memorial to the workers who tunnelled for three kilometres to drain water from the Crich lead mines.

A rare photograph of a working boat in action on the Cromford Canal. Dating from the early 20th century it shows a narrowboat, probably loaded with coal, heading north under Chase Bridge.

While their horse empties its nosebag, a team of council roadmen pose for the camera.

Public works helped the unemployment situation in the lean years after World War I. It's snap time !

A maintenance gang on the main line at Whatstandwell in the early 1930s.

Uniformed railway staff pose on the tracks between trains while the signalman stays dutifully in his box.

One of the oldest pictures in this collection shows Stephen Self in the livery of a boot boy in his early teens. He lived to be 102 and died at Sun Lane, Crich in 1957.

A beautifully turned-out horse and carriage stands at the door of Chase Cliffe, ready to do the bidding of the Hurt family.

Taken in the 1960s, this picture shows the framework knitters cottages on The Common built around 1790. Recent restoration has respected the appearance of this rare survivor.

The Hat Factory on Dimple Lane. Built in 1801 and intended for straw hat making, but hats may never have been made here. The Butterley Company bought the buildings in 1810 to house workers at the nearby Old Quarry. Originally built as two similar blocks, only the northern one now remains.

This grainy photograph shows the Bobbin Mill at Fritchley on the right. Powered by water from the impounded brook, production of wooden bobbins began here before 1820. A sawmill nearby was part of the integrated manufacturing process.

Another rare photograph of the Bobbin Mill (far left) before the fire.

The chimney in this picture of the Bobbin Mill indicates that a steam engine had been introduced to replace water power. But in 1885 the mill burned down and production was never resumed at this site.

The work force at Dawbarns pauses for a commemorative photo around 1930. Their plaque says "Yelverton Dawbarns Bros. Ltd. Steam Joinery Works". The firm produced window frames and doors and employed many people from the parish until the mid 1930s, when a major fire destroyed the works and stopped production.

A summer photo with Ambergate Woods as a background shows a group of workers at Johnson and Nephew Wireworks on the River Derwent. Production of heavy-gauge wire, barbed wire and associated products began in 1876 and continued for over a hundred years.

The Derwent Valley Water Board developed an ambitious project to impound the headwaters of the Derwent and transport water to Sheffield and southwards to Derby, Nottingham and Leicester. A major service reservoir, fed by pipelines from the Peak, perches on the high ground south of Crich. It holds 28 million gallons.

A photograph from May 1909 shows progress on the construction with roof beams in place. A roof was needed because the water arriving here had already been filtered and treated at Bamford.

Left: Once completed the reservoir was buttressed with earth and grassed over. It is known as the Ambergate Service Reservoir and is the second largest underground reservoir in the country.

Below: Just to the south of Chadwick Nick the Ilkeston and Heanor Water Board built another reservoir to hold water from the Homesford Works. With Crich Stand in the distance this picture shows men at work building the blue-brick vaults of a tank which has a capacity of 1.4 million gallons.

Right: In July 1903 photographs were taken to record progress at the site. Once in operation, water was transferred by gravity from Chadwick Nick to reservoirs at Codnor and Ilkeston.

A poignant photograph taken soon after the outbreak of World War I shows some of the youths of Crich who volunteered for action.

A few weeks later, the same group of lads are seen again in the uniform of the Sherwood Foresters with their officer, Captain MacDonald, son of the local doctor. This scene, captured in the garden at Rosskeen, was being repeated all over the country.

Two years into the War these two local men, photographed in France, look tired and battle-weary.

Left: On the Home Front the women worked too - a Whatstandwell girl is photographed in her nurses uniform.

Below: A sea of boater hats is in evidence as the predominantly female workforce at Lea Mills comes out on strike.

Happier times at Lea Mills in 1946 as the still predominantly female workforce gathers in the canteen for the BBC's 'Workers Playtime'.

Chaps from Crich and Fritchley are dotted amongst this team of workers photographed in 1937 at Stevensons Dye Works.

A wonderful Edwardian photograph shows a gallant band of ladies (and two men) on voluntary cleaning duty at Crich Church. The Reverend J. M. S. Simmons pretends to be in charge.

Family members and local worthies pose as Councillor Jim Briggs makes a presentation to well-known postman Ted Rollinson on the occasion of his retirement after many years of service in Crich.

The 'Top School' - Crich Church of England School - in the 1920s.

A photograph from the 1900s shows the infants at Crich Carr School with messages for posterity.

Taken on the same day with a group of older girls.

This is the Top School in 1922. The teachers are: Mrs. Else (left) and Miss Laughton (right).

A mixed group of infants at Crich Carr School circa 1926.

Many of the same faces appear in a photo from the following year.

This picture dates from about 1936 as Crich Carr schoolchildren put on a pageant for Empire Day.

There's no doubt about the date and place of this photograph !

The post-World War I baby boom, together with large families, meant large school
populations in the 1920s.

The cohort of children moves up through the school and the parents had to scrape-up the
money to buy an annual photograph.

It's a pity that the photographer stopped adding the date to his blackboard.

At Crich Carr the infants depart from the standard school photo by displaying some of their teaching aids.

Above: A happy class in the late 1930s.

Right: A more informal pose from the same period.

Left: A class of boys at Crich Carr Church of England School.

Les Barber is second-left on the front row. It still rankles with him that he was made to sit on a smaller chair than his mates and looks a bit of a weed in comparison !

A nice picture from 1952 of Whatstandwell and Crich Carr children.

In the playing field at Crich 'Bottom School' in 1952. The teacher, Mr. Flory,
supervises a roguish Standard Three.

This photograph (the original in colour) was from the 1960s when school colour photos first appeared.

Infants and juniors comprising the whole of a much smaller school population at
Crich Carr School in the 1960s.

Bringing this section to a close, an indoor photo from about 1970. The school for Whatstandwell
maintains its name as Crich Carr C of E School to the present day.

Above: A Victorian photograph shows the great and the good of Derbyshire assembled at Chase Cliffe as guests of the Hurt sisters. The Hurt family had the house built in 1860.

Left: Workers at Lea Mills celebrate an important episode in the Boer War - the Relief of Mafeking in 1900.

A charming picture of a Whatstandwell choir in 1907.

A Crich-born coachman called Wragg seems to be giving joy rides to village worthies in the Duke of Devonshire's coach. Did the Duke know ?

A familiar postcard showing Crich Fair on the Market Place in 1908.

The garden at Fernside, Fritchley in September 1907 as relatives and friends gather for a Quaker wedding. Arthur Ludlow married Catherine Sargent Smith at the nearby Friends Meeting House.

Whatstandwell Brass Band, mostly in uniform, pose for a group photo in the 1920s.

This scene shows the Band as part of a carnival procession coming over Whatstandwell Bridge –
playing as they march. PC Breed, the local bobby, keeps order.

A Whitsuntide parade in Edwardian times passes the Co-op shop on Crich Common.

The Crich Band is engulfed by this crowd on the Market Place.

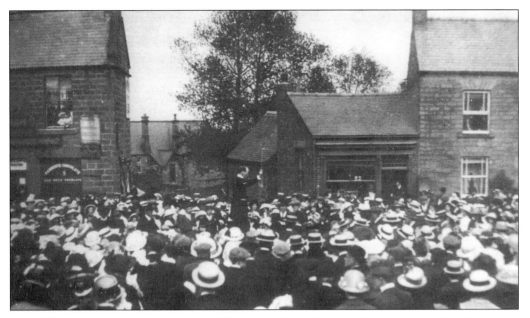

Joseph Haywood, headmaster at the Top School, was always known affectionately as 'Daddy'. In a view taken about 1908 he is conducting the singing on the Market Place.

A photograph taken on the same occasion, probably a Chapel Anniversary, shows that the assembly has reached Snowdrop Valley and are again in full voice.

In the early 1920s another crowd gathers on the Market Place. Silhouetted against the advertisements, Daddy Haywood is either conducting or orating.

From a vantage point near the Kings Arms the photographer captures a patriotic parade in the Edwardian era.

With bunting decorating the houses at the top of Bowns Hill, it seems very likely that this picture captures a victory parade at the end of World War I.

The presence of a soldier on this float outside the Red Lion, Fritchley also suggests a victory celebration.

From the parapet of Crich Top School a photographer captures this march-past by a Boy Scout troop. Rumour persists that the adult in the lead is a Miss Hammond !

A fundraising event at Chase Cliffe brings out costumes and spotless aprons; proceeds to the Red Cross.

Again the Top School provides a grandstand for this parade in the early 1920s.

Whatstandwell musters a modest carnival procession in the 1920s.

Later in the 1920s floats and banners are captured at the foot of Bennetts Lane.

In 1923 gypsies and witches allow themselves to be photographed at Crich Carnival.

In 1927 a bevy of local beauties graces a decorated float on Crich Market Place.

The costumes are getting very elaborate at this Whatstandwell carnival in the late 1920s.

Even the
perambulators have
gone over the top !
Did it win a prize ?

The wedding was held at Crich Church but the guests returned to Crich Carr School for the reception and this happy, informal picture.

A visit by the Christian evangelist, Mr. Frank Penfold, is commemorated in this photo of his marquee erected in the Jovial Dutchman croft.

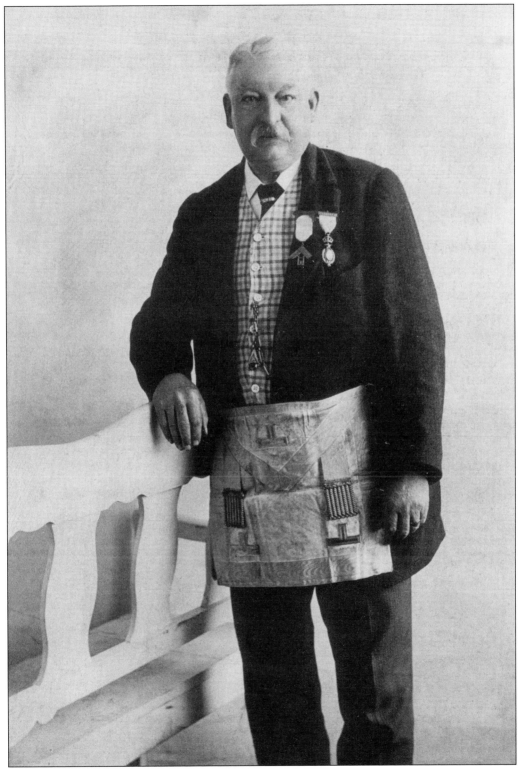

John Dawes of Crich poses in his regalia of the 'Order of Druids'.

An elaborate float at the 1929 Crich Carnival.

A char-a-banc trip to the seaside around 1930. The vehicle was owned by
Les 'Basher' Smith and he called it 'Dora'.

Another generation of schoolchildren keep up the tradition of pageants at Crich Carr School.

As floats assemble in the Market Place for the 1938 carnival, a group of 'Spaniards' pose for the camera.

The occupants of this float look less thrilled about being photographed than the previous bunch !

A large proportion of Fritchley's population assembles on The Green for this carnival event.

The Crich Scout Troop is let loose on Paignton in the summer of 1938. Scoutmaster Reg Page (left), a well-known local figure, looks on benignly.

Crich Walking Club pose in the Peak District in about 1939. The bearded figure is Arthur Watkins, an amateur local historian. The balding man near the rock face is W. H. Emmas-Williams, local headmaster and later a local councillor.

Above: Who could resist the Red Cross collecting tins in the hands of these Whatstandwell young ladies in 1945 ?

Left: Before setting-off from Thurlow Booth to Whatstandwell Carnival.

It's the late 1940s, and a smiling group line up for a photograph in the yard of the Wheatsheaf at Whatstandwell. The licensee, Billy Bowmer, is on the left of those sitting on the flagstones.

The early 1950s and local ladies are happy to sprint over tussocky grass in a race at Crich Carnival.

It's Coronation year and the flower of Crich's womanhood is transformed for a day into Carnival 'Royalty'. Note the purpose-built float with unmissable loudspeakers.

A rare picture shows the inside of the Parish Room in 1955 as the senior citizens enjoy their Christmas party. Sitting at centre stage is Stephen Self, who at 100 was Crich's oldest inhabitant.

The Crich Players were formed in May 1952 and took to the boards at both Crich Cinema on The Common and at the Top School.

The players mounted their first production in November 1952; here they are staging "Russian Salad"

George Oliver's bass drum keeps time as the Wesleyan Methodist Sunday School engages in the Whitsun procession of 1950 along Bulling Lane.

Weak May sunshine lights-up the banners as the churches keep up the Whitsun tradition in 1959.

The ladies of Whatstandwell Women's Institute pose for the camera before heading-off on an outing by rail.

Willingly ambushed by the resident photographer at Trentham Gardens near Stoke, a large party from Fritchley Chapel arrange themselves on the steps in the late 1940s.

The self-same steps at Trentham Gardens in about 1953, but this time mainly Whatstandwell folk with a sprinkling of faces from Crich.

Reg and Olive Page emerge from their wedding at Crich Church to find a Scouts' guard of honour.

The tradition lives on at the June 1969 wedding of Stephen Dawes and Diana Hall.

Dr. John Twist presides over the balloon launch; he was the local GP for many years from the 1940s to the 1970s. The occasion is a fundraising event at Chase Cliffe in aid of the Church Restoration appeal.

The belles of Crich cremate sausages at a barbecue event in aid of the Scout Hut Fund held at Crich Recreation Ground in 1963.

A parade of Scouts and friends winds its way along Jeffries Lane.   *G. Smith*

After years of fundraising the new Scout Hut on Jeffries Lane is built and is to be shared with the Guides. This photograph from 1965 shows the official opening. On the left of the three churchmen is the Reverend Gordon Bathie, then Vicar of Crich.

Fritchley Women's Institute was formed in 1923. Here the ladies gather at the top of Bull Bridge Hill to hand over a newly-funded seat to the Parish Council.

Crich United Silver Prize Band, formed in 1900, is photographed outside the Baptist Chapel. At Christmas 1964 it toured the village playing carols – its last appearance before disbanding.   *G. Smith*

The Fritchley branch of St. Trinians - otherwise known as the W.I. - get up to their old and new tricks in the schoolroom of the Congregational Chapel.

In September 1985 a pageant was devised and staged at Crich Church to celebrate its 850th anniversary as a place of worship.

Crich Brigade Football Club in the 1904-05 season.

Crich Cricket Club was formed in the 1860s but this photo only goes back to the 1920s.

The cricket team of the 1920s was good enough to win trophies.

Later in the 1920s new blood has come in but some of the veterans are still playing. The pitch was sited off the Market Place, to the rear of the Mansion House.

Whatstandwell Swifts Football Club in the 1920-21 season.

Whatstandwell Rovers Football Club in the 1922-23 season.

Whatstandwell Football Club played in the Third Division of the Matlock and District League, winning the Divisional Cup in 1923.

Crich Rangers were also collecting trophies at that time, displaying them here in the yard of the Bulls Head.

Crich Church of England School team in 1926-27, producing the stars of tomorrow. 'Daddy' Haywood keeps an eye on things.

A rival team of youngsters at the Crich Carr School.

The landlord and landlady of the Wheatsheaf, Whatstandwell proudly pose with the local team in the pub yard circa 1935.

The Wheatsheaf had changed hands by 1940 and the pub darts team poses on the much-photographed flagstones.

A Whatstandwell team in the 1944-45 season.

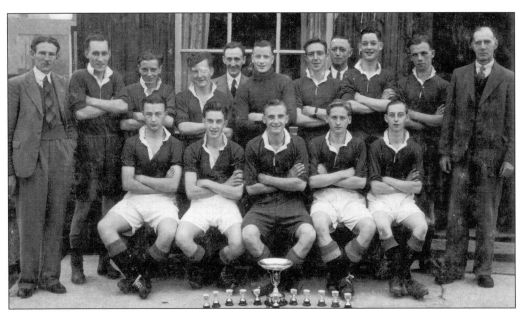

A trophy-winning team with both Crich and Whatstandwell youths poses by the wooden tearooms at Town End, Crich.

Crich Rangers in 1947-48. The Bulls Head was their base and they then trotted to a field at the bottom of Stand Lane to play.

Some changes of personnel, but in 1951 Crich Rangers still had winning talents.

A Stevensons Dye Works football team from about 1960.

Percy Smith, sitting in the centre, captained this 1940s Crich cricket team and is to be seen in the team photos from the 1920s.

A Whatstandwell cricket team with more than enough white flannels to field eleven men.

A Crich Cricket Club team in 1960 - they often had to draft in youngsters to make-up the numbers !

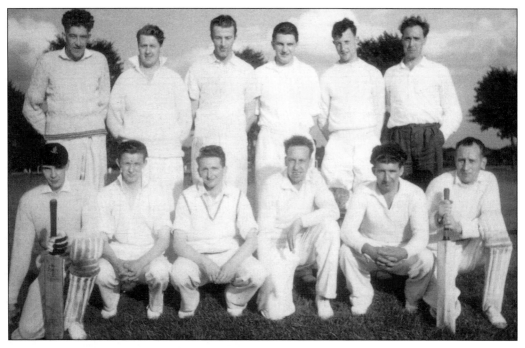

A Whatstandwell team in the early 1960s.

In the 1930s, the Crich Cricket Club moved from its pitch in the heart of the village to a field on the outskirts, with the strange name of Top Doctor. What it gained in extensive views, it lost in community support.

The Club soldiered on until 1963 and is seen here in its last season.